Mastering Media

Social Networks and Blogs

Lori Hile

www.raintreepublishers.co.uk
Visit our website to find out
more information about
Raintree books.

To order:
☎ Phone 0845 6044371
🖹 Fax +44 (0) 1865 312263
🖳 Email myorders@raintreepublishers.co.uk

Customers from outside the UK please telephone +44 1865 312262

Raintree is an imprint of Capstone Global Library
Limited, a company incorporated in England and
Wales having its registered office at 7 Pilgrim
Street, London, EC4V 6LB
– Registered company number: 6695582

Edited by Adam Miller, Andrew Farrow,
  and Adrian Vigliano
Designed by Steve Mead
Original illustrations © Capstone Global
  Library Ltd
Picture research by Elizabeth Alexander
Originated by Capstone Global Library Ltd
Printed in China by South China Printing
  Company Ltd

ISBN 978 1 406 21762 9 (hardback)
14 13 12 11 10
10 9 8 7 6 5 4 3 2 1

British Library Cataloguing in Publication Data

Hile, Lori
Social networks and blogs. – (Mastering media)
006.7'54-dc22
A full catalogue record for this book is available
from the British Library.

Acknowledgements

We would like to thank the following for permission
to reproduce photographs: © 2010 Last.fm Ltd
p. **35**; Alamy pp. **4** (© UpperCut Images), **8** (©
Galen Rowell/Mountain Light), **12** (© isifa Image
Service s.r.o.), **17** (© CJG – Technology), **18** (©
Richard Wareham Fotografie), **28** (© TomBham);
Corbis pp. **14** (© Bumper DeJesus/Star Ledger),
19 (© Dziekan/Retna Ltd.), **27 bottom** (© Rob Kim/
Retna Ltd.), **27 top** (© Andy Warhol Foundation),
31 (© HO/Reuters), **41** (© Sion Touhig), **42** (©
C.J. Burton), **44** (© Patrik Giardino), **45** (© Jared
Milgrim); Getty Images pp. **6** (WireImage/
Tony Barson), **10** (Joe Raedle), **15** (Lifesize/Jetta
Productions), **20** (Steven Hunt), **25** (Michael
Reynolds-Pool), **33** (Yellow Dog Productions),
36 (Jeff J Mitchell), **46** (SHADISHD173/AFP);
iStockphoto p. **34** (© Jane Norton); Nasim Fekrat
www.afghanlord.org p. **7**; Press Association
Images p. **23** (Adrian Wyld/The Canadian Press);
Provided by the Metropolitan Police Service p. **39**;
Shutterstock pp. **22** (© Miodrag Gajic), **30** (© Steve
Smith); © The Royal Channel p. **38**.

Cover photograph of crowd of young adults taking
photos of man with mobile phones, reproduced
with permission of Getty Images/Mike Powell/
Stone+.

The author thanks Elizabeth Hubbard and all of the
young people she gathered in her home, for their
input and insights. A special thanks to Maggie Lott
and Noah Eisfelder.

We would like to thank Devorah Heitner for her
invaluable help in the preparation of this book.

Every effort has been made to contact copyright
holders of material reproduced in this book. Any
omissions will be rectified in subsequent printings
if notice is given to the publisher.

Disclaimer

Contents

Some words are printed in bold, **like this**. You can find out what they mean by looking in the glossary.

Digital
democracy

Young people with Internet access can make their voices heard.

You are whisked aboard a time machine and transported back to the year 1990. You are placed in front of a computer, logged on to the Internet, and asked to find a video of a popular entertainer. Can you do it? Chances are, you will not even recognise what you see in front of you.

You look for a search engine, but Yahoo!, Google, and Bing have not been invented yet. You browse for pictures or videos, but you find mostly black and white text. This is because photos and videos take up too much memory for the Internet to handle. You try to chat with friends, but you find yourself alone. Most families do not own computers.

The Internet: it's all about you!

Let's hop back to the present time. You can easily "surf" the Internet because search engines have been invented and refined. You will see lots of colourful videos and pictures, because computers and the Internet have a lot more room for memory. Perhaps the biggest change, however, is the way today's technology allows you to interact with the features you see.

This "new and improved" Internet is often called **Web 2.0**. On today's Internet, you can do more than just read an article. You can write your own. You can do more than just read about a film. You can watch one. Or you can make your own film, then **post** it (transfer it from your computer) on the Internet for instant feedback. You can do more than just read an encyclopedia entry. You can also change the information you find in it.

The key word here is *you*. Have you ever heard your parents or friends say, "It's not always about you"? Well, in the case of Web 2.0, they are wrong. Internet **media**, as they exist today, are all about you. These media are all about the way ordinary people like you interact with and shape them. In fact, *Time* magazine chose "You" as "Person of the Year" in 2006 for that reason. Congratulations!

Case studies: citizen journalism

Here are some examples of the ways in which citizens like you have been able to use Internet media to get their voices heard:

French hip-hop artist Kamini.

Kamini's story

Kamini, 29, grew up in Marly-Gomont, a tiny French town. Kamini always received attention, partly because he was black in a mostly white village, and partly because he listened to rap music. He liked to rap himself, and he wrote about what he knew: cows, mopeds, and racism.

In August 2006 he made a video of his music, posted it **online**, and emailed a number of record labels to let them know. One record label posted the video on a small site that had nothing to do with music (it sold T-shirts). Kamini's music was listened to anyway and was then posted on YouTube and other video sites. By mid-October, all the interest in his music had landed him a contract with a major record label.

Nasim's story

Nasim Fekrat, 26, was raised in a small village in Afghanistan by his very religious Muslim family. (Muslims are believers in the religion of **Islam**.) When Nasim was 11, he was thrown out of the house for refusing to pray.

He slept on the roof for several nights. Then he followed a group of people who were fleeing to Pakistan, Iran, and the United Arab Emirates. In these neighbouring countries, Nasim read every book he could find and began teaching himself English. Nasim also discovered Afghan poetry and classical music. He wanted to share these art forms with the world.

"Afghan Lord" blogger Nasim Fekrat teaches young Afghans how to blog, so they can express their thoughts about living in Afghanistan.

Later, Nasim moved back to Afghanistan. In 2004 he started a **blog** called "Afghan Lord". Nasim uses both English and his native Farsi to show readers that there is more to Afghanistan than violence, poverty, and disease, even in the midst of a war. Nasim also runs a blogging school, where he teaches young Afghans about media and technology so that they have, in his words, "powerful tools to write about … society".

New voices

Twenty years ago, Kamini's and Nasim's stories might not have been possible. Neither Kamini nor Nasim had a lot of money or power. What they did have was a vision – and access to Internet media. Today, almost anyone with Internet access can get his or her voice heard. The more voices we hear, the fuller the picture we have of the world around us. That is why it is so important to learn what tools the Internet has to offer, so that you, too, can participate in the conversation.

Blogging and micro-blogging

Blogs allow readers a glimpse into unfamiliar parts of the world, such as the South Pole.

THE UNITED STATES OF AMERICA
WELCOMES YOU TO
AMUNDSEN - SCOTT SOUTH POLE STATION

Have you ever wondered what it would be like to live on the South Pole? Twenty years ago, you would have to hop on a plane or wait until a **journalist** (reporter) published an article or made a television programme about it. Now, you can just visit one of several "Antarctica" **blogs** to learn more about living on our coldest continent, and you can even watch a video taken from a camera mounted in a weather station.

The evolution of blogs

A "blog" (short for "weblog") is an **online** journal that looks like a web page, with the most recent entries on top. Most blogs also allow readers to **post** their own comments. On a South Pole blog, for instance, a reader could ask questions about weather conditions or share their own wintry experiences. What makes blogs different from websites is that they are much easier to create and update with text, photos, and links to other sites. This means almost anyone with Internet access can create a blog and instantly communicate his or her thoughts.

Before blogs, it was hard to find certain kinds of information about a topic all in one place on the Internet. Aside from publishing a book or magazine, it was difficult for the average person to share information with a worldwide audience. As Internet technology became more **interactive**, blogs were born. In 1999 a company called Pyra Labs introduced a free weblog publishing tool called "Blogger" to the public.

In 1999 there were about 50 blogs. In 2004 there were 4.1 million blogs. By 2008 there were roughly 112.8 million blogs. You can now find blogs on almost any topic. There are thousands of entertainment blogs, medical blogs, sports blogs, environmental blogs, current events blogs, and travel blogs. You can start your own blog about whatever you like.

Blogging detectives

In 2005, 19-year-old Kaavya Viswanathan, a student from Harvard University in the United States, published her first novel, *How Opal Mehta Got Kissed, Got Wild, and Got a Life*. The book featured a bright young Indian-American girl who applies to Harvard, only to be told she is too studious. So, Opal begins to behave more like a typical teenager. Viswanathan's publisher, Little, Brown, liked the book so much it asked her to write a second novel.

Then, in 2006, the Harvard newspaper accused Viswanathan of a few examples of **plagiarism** (copying someone else's work). After her story was reported in major news outlets, bloggers collected and presented evidence that she had actually copied more than 40 paragraphs, nearly word-for-word, from six different novels. In light of this proof, her publisher took Viswanathan's books off the shelves and cancelled her second book contract.

> Kaavya Viswanathan's novel was removed from shops after her plagiarism was discovered.

Ways to use blogs

Blogs are used for many different purposes today. For example, many television networks ask viewers to share their thoughts and photos on blog sites. These viewers' words and images are seen by other viewers or even broadcast on television.

Some universities are including student blogs on their official websites. This allows 6th form and college pupils to get first-hand accounts of university life from students, rather than school officials.

Blogs can also help expose errors or lies told by individuals, government agencies, or the **mainstream media** (sources such as major newspapers that present commonly accepted views).

Blogs are also used by lots of young people. Of all the blogs produced, half are written by people between the ages of 13 and 19. About 20 per cent of US teenagers read blogs, and 23 per cent of teenagers who read blogs also publish their own.

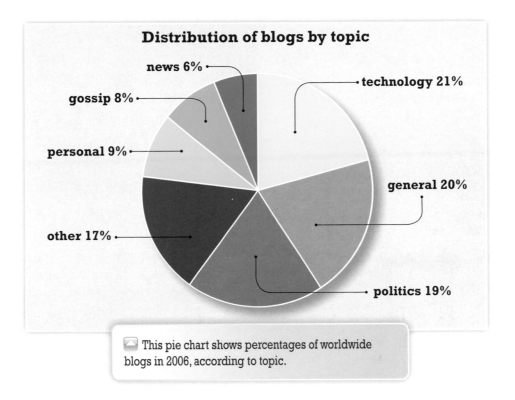

Distribution of blogs by topic

news 6%
technology 21%
gossip 8%
personal 9%
general 20%
other 17%
politics 19%

This pie chart shows percentages of worldwide blogs in 2006, according to topic.

Drawbacks of blogs

While blogs provide a lot of useful information, they also present problems. For example, journalists are trained to observe certain rules and standards. On the other hand, anyone can write a blog, which means there are often errors of fact or judgement. Unlike newspapers, magazines, and television stations, blogs do not have editors and fact-checkers to double check their information.

Bloggers can also print information that is crude, racist, or **pornographic** (sexually explicit). For these reasons, many people believe that blogs need more regulation. However, some bloggers believe that rules will limit their freedom of speech. Also, blog regulations are hard to enforce, since bloggers can keep their identities secret and can create blogs from anywhere in the world.

Tips for evaluating blogs and websites

Since no one is monitoring the quality of blogs, you must do it yourself. Here are some questions to help you decide how to evaluate the usefulness and accuracy of a blog or other website.

Who wrote the entry?

Does the author provide a biography or contact information? If the author is anonymous, why do you think this person is keeping his or her identity private? Does the author or organization represent a particular point of view? For instance, a blog published by the Humane Society will probably express a very different viewpoint on animal rights than a blog written by a hunting club.

What is the purpose of the blog?

Why did someone create this blog? To entertain? To educate? To push a particular point of view or product? Web addresses that end with ".com" (meaning "commercial business") or ".net" are

Not all blogs are created equal, so it is important to think critically about the information found in blogs and websites.

often commercial websites selling a product or brand. Addresses that end in ".edu", ".gov", ".mil", or ".org" are usually non-commercial or non-profit sites, meant to educate or advance a cause.

When was the blog posted?

It may take a little hunting to find out when the blog was created, but it is important to know whether the information you are reading is updated or outdated.

Where does a blogger get his or her facts?

Sometimes bloggers get their information from other websites or blogs, which may not be reliable themselves. Track down the original source of the information. Then, see how it compares with other blogs, websites, or articles on the same topic.

Are there grammatical mistakes or misspellings?

Nobody is perfect, but you have to wonder: if an author cannot be bothered to spell-check, can he or she be trusted to fact-check?

Does the author use neutral words?

How do the author's word choices seem to you? Are they neutral, or do the words seem intended to provoke an emotional response? For instance, an article could say that the government is "robbing" taxpayers. Unless the government is literally pick-pocketing its citizens, the word *robbing* is being used simply to sway the reader's feelings about the issue.

The bottom line is that, just as you do not trust every person you meet, you should not trust every blog you read.

See how they've grown

As blogging has grown, the length of the average blog has kept shrinking. Thanks to **micro-blogging** tools like text messages and Twitter (see pages 14 to 19), short blogs have also become big business.

Blog "netiquette"

The Internet may seem less "real" than life, but people should follow the same standards of behaviour as they do in real life. Online comments can still hurt people's feelings or damage their reputation. If bloggers write something untrue about someone, they could even be breaking the law. Bloggers should also avoid "flaming" (talking angrily) or "SHOUTING" (talking in all caps). Always remember to think before you post!

TXT MSGS in the classroom

Does your "BFF" (best friend forever) make you "LOL" (laugh out loud)? Many young people use abbreviations like these when texting, since mobile phone keypads are small and messages are kept short.

Text abbreviations are fine for casual conversations with friends. But sometimes young people forget and use them for class assignments. Most teachers do not accept this kind of language and will mark points off for "misspelling" if students continue to use them.

It is helpful to remember that text messaging is like a whole separate "language", one with different rules for spelling, punctuation, and grammar. It is important to follow the proper rules when writing, so that you will be clearly understood by all your readers. You would not use Spanish words in your English classroom, so do not use the language of texting there, either.

Another thing to avoid in the classroom is sending text messages. This behaviour is always rude, because it shows your teachers that you are not paying attention. A teacher might even take your phone away for the day.

Ways to use texting

Have you ever sent a text message on a mobile phone? If so, you are a "micro-blogger"! A micro-blog is simply a short blog. Text messages are short, since most phones limit the number of characters you can use. In fact, the official term for "text messaging" is "*SMS*", which stands for "short message system".

Besides talking on the phone, texting is the most popular way for young people to communicate. These are some of the reasons young people say they like to text:

- You can text from anywhere.
- Almost everyone has a mobile phone, even if they do not have an email address or belong to a social network like Facebook.
- You can send a message when you cannot, or do not want to, talk to someone, and you can respond to a message whenever you want.

Don't try this at school!

Texting in the media

Young people primarily send text messages to friends and family, but texting can also be a powerful and fun way to get your voice heard by the mainstream media. Television programmes such as *Strictly Come Dancing* ask viewers to vote for performers by either calling or texting a certain number.

Many television news broadcasts use texting as a quick way to see what viewers are thinking. This allows them to get a quick "poll" result, and it allows viewers to express their opinions. Of course, since the same person can vote many times, these results are not always fair or accurate.

> Studies have found that many young people text thousands of times per month.

Drawbacks of texting

Texting can be a great communication tool, but it is not appropriate – or safe – in every situation. Keep in mind the following important cautions:

- Texting while walking can be dangerous, and texting while cycling or driving is always dangerous.
- Text-messaging plans often have a monthly limit. Find out your limit, and do not go over it! You or your parents might have to pay an "overage" fee.
- You can never be sure if the person you are texting is the person actually receiving your texts, since you cannot hear a voice or see a face. Sometimes friends text from their friends' phones. So be careful what you text.
- When you talk in person, you communicate with your face and tone of voice. When texting, you can only use words. If you are not careful, your words might not come across in the way you intended. "Emoticons" like smiley faces can go a long way towards communicating a friendly tone. :)

Micro-blogging: a brief history of Twitter

Imagine that you just won tickets to see your favourite band. You are very excited, so you immediately want to share the news with everyone you know. You pull out your mobile phone but cannot easily text more than one person at once. You could update your blog, but people might not read it for days.

This is where micro-blogging sites like Twitter come in handy. On Twitter, you can send out

Did you know?

The very first text message, "Merry Christmas", was sent by an engineer in December 1992. However, texting did not become popular with the general public until almost a decade later. In 2000, 17 billion text messages were sent. People sent 250 billion text messages one year later. By 2008, people sent over 1 trillion text messages!

short blog posts to a group of people in "real time". The founders of Twitter designed the site to help friends and family keep in touch through the exchange of frequent, live updates.

Twitter messages, known as "**tweets**", appear on the user's home page and are delivered to the user's "followers". Followers could be friends, family, or fans – anyone who signs up to receive the user's "tweets". Some people use Twitter on their computers, but many people "tweet" on the go. The founders deliberately limited the messages to 140 characters so they could be sent over mobile phones. There are a few other micro-blogging sites, but Twitter is currently the most popular. It is also one of the 50 most popular websites in the world.

A little bird told me

"Tweets" were given their name by Twitter users, rather than the founders of the company.

Many young people use Twitter to send **status updates** and follow celebrities.

Ways to use Twitter

The founders of Twitter soon learned that the site could be used for more than just communication between family and friends.

When Twitter first went "live" in 2006, all three Twitter founders felt a small earthquake in San Francisco, USA. They immediately tweeted about it and noticed that other Twitter users were already doing the same thing. They checked several mainstream media outlets, but none had announced the quake yet. This made Twitter's founders realize that Twitter could be a tool to help break the news. Here are some others ways that micro-blogging is used:

- As a marketing tool
  Businesses send Twitter messages to make crowds gather at last-minute events or sales.
- As an organizing tool
  In April 2009, citizens in the eastern European country of Moldova used Twitter to encourage more than 10,000 young people to protest against the country's new **communist** leaders. (Communism is a political system in which a country's economy is controlled by the government.)

Protesters in Moldova used Twitter to organize huge, anti-communist **rallies** like this one.

- As an emergency tool
  In February 2009, devastating bushfires swept through the Australian state of Victoria. Australian Prime Minister Kevin Rudd used Twitter to let residents know where to seek emergency help and how to donate money and blood.
- As a celebrity mouthpiece
  Many celebrities love Twitter because they know that their "tweets" will keep them in the minds of their "followers". They hope this results in sales of their new albums or films. Also, many celebrity gossip magazines and websites say things about celebrities that are exaggerated or false. Twitter allows celebrities to control their own images by speaking directly to fans.

Micro-blogging drawbacks

Twitter can spread news fast, but it can spread rumours just as quickly. After the deaths of celebrities Michael Jackson and Farrah Fawcett on 25 June 2009, someone relayed a rumour on Twitter that a third celebrity, actor Jeff Goldblum, had also died while filming a film in New Zealand. No one was more surprised to hear this than Jeff Goldblum, who was alive and well in Los Angeles, USA!

Twitter can also distract you from more important things. Do you really need to know what your best friend had for lunch, especially if you ate it with her in the canteen?

Join the micro revolution

You, too, can join Twitter and find your own "followers". You can also "follow" whomever you would like, even famous people. Just be careful, as you do not want to risk having someone "follow" you around in real life. (See page 43 for more Internet safety tips.)

A smiling Jeff Goldblum proves that rumours of his death were greatly exaggerated.

Cyber communities

The Internet can be a confusing and seemingly endless place. Sometimes you just want to go where everybody knows your name – or user ID. **Web portals** provide a familiar place in a sea of information. Social-networking sites offer a base for reaching out to friends.

Web portals

A web portal combines information from different places on one page. You will find email, instant messaging (IM) programs (see below), search engines (like Google or Yahoo!), and news of your choosing, all on your "home page". Examples of free, public web portal sites include MSN, Yahoo!, AOL, and iGoogle.

Email

Email (short for "electronic mail") is a method for exchanging **digital** messages with other people. Unlike text messages, which come from mobile phones, emails can be exchanged and stored on the Internet, or on your computer. Email has no character limit, which makes it a good way to communicate formal information.

Many young people now prefer sending messages via social networks (see pages 22 and 23), but email allows you to reach people who are not members of your social network. It can be a good way to connect with distant friends and family.

However, users should be careful not to trust email messages from people they do not know. Often these are scams or unwanted advertisements called spam.

Instant messages

Most email programs offer IM utilities that allow people to exchange messages over the Internet in "real time". After one person sends a message, it pops up in a little bubble on the other person's page. This is a popular way for young people to communicate, since almost everyone has email and IM capabilities. However, keep in mind that IMing is not appropriate for formal communications with teachers or some adults.

What are social networks?

After she logs on to her computer, Maggie, 13, goes straight to her social-networking page. Maggie is not alone. Facebook, the most popular social-networking site, is the fourth-most-visited website in the world.

Young people flock to social-networking sites in order to connect or reconnect with friends.

Like web portals, social-networking sites offer email and IMing. They also allow you to **upload** a picture of yourself, create a "profile" describing your interests, and become "friends" with other users. You can **post blogs** or short "**status updates**", which appear on your profile page and on your friends' home pages. Social-networking sites have only been popular since about 2005, but they are changing the ways people communicate news and information. People use social-networking sites like Facebook and Bebo to "scoop" the **mainstream media**, meaning they try to break news stories first. For example, in May 2008, when a powerful earthquake struck China, people began "Facebooking" about it as quickly as they could, in an attempt to break the story first. In the end however, Twitter users broke the story first.

Users also often discuss and post pictures of sporting events, political debates, or celebrity meltdowns before the details have been published elsewhere. Social-networking sites often serve as **virtual** communities for people to reflect on events after they occur. For instance, after Haiti was devastated by an earthquake in January 2010, many Facebook pages were created so that supporters could share photos, thoughts, and ways to help victims.

People around the world have tried to use social networks to help Haiti as it recovers from the January 2010 earthquake.

The number-one reason young people give for joining social networks is that it allows them to connect with friends. Many people also like the way they can present a particular image of themselves on a social network.

Choosing a social network

Some of the most popular social networks include Facebook, MySpace, Tagged, and Bebo. The names may have changed by the time you read this, but chances are, social networks are here to stay. So, choose the site where most of your friends and family are already members. However, remember that on most social networks, you must be at least 13 years old to join.

Socialise safely

Using social networks can be a lot of fun, but keep the following safety tips in mind:

- **"Friend" or foe?**
  It is hard to resist a "friend request," but it is smart to "friend" only real friends or people you have already met. If someone gets in touch with you and makes you feel uncomfortable, block that person and tell an adult.
- **Don't gossip**
  Social networks are a great place to express yourself, but be careful about what you say. Some young people have been suspended for posting mean or untrue things about classmates or teachers.
- **Think before you post**
  Always ask yourself: would my friend want me to post this picture of him or her or to tell this story?
- **A picture is worth…**
  Some companies sell photos from the Internet to advertising agencies. Many social-networking users are surprised to find their own photo staring back at them in ads. If your photos are used inappropriately, contact your social network.
- Privacy
  Ask yourself: whom do I want viewing my profile? A "high privacy" setting means that only friends can see your information. A "low privacy" setting means that anyone can see it, even complete strangers. When in doubt, choose the highest setting.

For more Internet safety tips, see page 43.

❝ First of all, I want everybody here to be careful about what you post on Facebook – because in the YouTube age, whatever you do, it will be pulled up again later somewhere in your life. And when you're young, you make mistakes and you do some stupid stuff. And I've been hearing a lot about young people who – you know, they're posting stuff on Facebook, and then suddenly they go apply for a job and somebody has done a search and [they find some bad stuff about you] – so that's some practical political advice for you right there. That's number one. **❞**

– US President Barack Obama, 8 September 2009, answering a pupil who asked about how he could become president one day

📄 Since an increasing number of employers check social- networking sites before hiring, it pays to listen to President Obama's advice.

The parent (or grandparent) trap

As more and more adults join social-networking sites like Facebook, more and more young people are receiving "friend" requests from parents and even grandparents. This is great news for some, who welcome the chance to stay in touch with parents and other relatives. Others are not so keen. These teenagers enjoy having their own space, away from the prying eyes of adults.

What can you do? Your parents, being your parents, do have a right and responsibility to see what you are posting. They can even help you make better decisions. For instance, one 13-year-old boy posted a joke about his teacher. His friends thought it was funny, but his dad saw the remark and reminded his son that he could get in trouble for it at school. The boy thought about it and removed the post.

Some things young people say about social networking:

> " Facebook is good for seeing what's up, to catch up on what people have been doing if you haven't talked to them. But you don't get personal communication [with Facebook]. You can find out everything without talking to them, but you *should* talk to them, have a conversation with them. "
>
> – Noah, 13

> " Sometimes there's a lot of drama [on social-networking sites]. People can be more open online. It's easier to type than talk, and you don't have to look at the person. "
>
> – Maggie, 13

Fifteen minutes of fame

Artist Andy Warhol famously declared in 1968, "In the future, everyone will be world famous for 15 minutes". That future is now. The popularity of reality television programmes like *Big Brother* have made "stars" of average citizens. The tools available on today's Internet allow almost everyone to broadcast their own profile or video to as many as two billion viewers worldwide. Many people share their private thoughts on blogs or micro-blogs and post their pictures for the world to see.

Most people don't become world famous, but their lives are a lot less private than when Andy Warhol was alive.

There is a dark side to all of this instant "fame". Some fear that people will do almost anything – even dangerous or bad things – just to get their "15 minutes" and may regret their actions after they have had time to think. Some say that this type of "fame" is really just another way of saying "the end of privacy".

Pop quiz: do you know the names of these "15 minutes" celebrities? If you do, how much time do you think they have left in the spotlight?

Cyber-sharing: wikis and ratings

It takes a lot of people working together to create a wiki.

English
e Free Encyclopedia
2 904 000+ articles

utsch
Enzyklopädie
000+ Artikel

ais
die libre
articles

Italiano
ciclopedia libera
574 000+ voci

Русский
педия

A wiki is a website that is created in collaboration with other people. On a wiki site, visitors can change whatever they want, whenever they want. This is different from a **blog**, where users can make comments but cannot change what the blog author has already written. On a wiki site, users can actually write over someone else's words. In this way, wiki sites allow groups of people to create projects or documents together, similar to the way many groups work together in scientific fields and businesses.

The most famous wiki "project" is Wikipedia, an **interactive**, **online** encyclopedia (see pages 30 and 31). Wikis are also cropping up in schools and businesses. These wikis are usually closed to the public and require an invitation to participate.

For example, one Year Five science teacher created a private wiki site called "Inventa-pedia" to get her pupils thinking about inventions for their annual science fair. When pupils logged on to the wiki, they saw a home page with photos of past fairs and reminders about due dates and guidelines. Pupils could also click on a "discussion board" page to write questions and share ideas with others. Pupils were free to contribute to the site whenever and wherever they wanted, even from home.

The teacher was surprised by the results. Within a day of launching the site, every single pupil had written at least one comment, even though participation was not required. The teacher noticed that many of her pupils were working on the project late into the night and even on weekends. Together, the pupils worked so hard and generated so many ideas that they finished their projects two weeks faster than any class in the past. The teacher also found that many of the quietest pupils in class asked the most questions and provided the most suggestions online. The wiki allowed all the pupils to benefit from each other's ideas, which benefitted the project as a whole.

Wikipedia versus *Encyclopaedia Britannica*

In 2005 the science journal *Nature* pitted Wikipedia against *Encyclopaedia Britannica,* the oldest and most trusted encyclopedia in the English language. The challenge was to see which one was more accurate on a range of scientific topics. Experts judged 42 different entries. The results were that there were an average of four errors in each Wikipedia entry and three in each *Britannica* entry. The reviewers also found a total of eight "serious errors". Four of these were from Wikipedia entries, four from *Britannica* entries.

This study surprised a lot of people. Even though *Britannica's* contributors have included famous scientists such as Albert Einstein and Carl Sagan, Wikipedia's science entries in the sample were almost as accurate. Although each encyclopedia collects its information differently, the study shows that both approaches can produce good information.

How does Wikipedia stack up against *Encyclopaedia Britannica?*

Advantages of Wikipedia

Launched in January 2001, the English-language version of Wikipedia contains over 3 million entries on a wide range of topics. That is more than any other encyclopedia – online or off-line. Wikipedia is the most popular general reference work on the Internet and among the 10 most popular websites worldwide.

What makes Wikipedia different from other encyclopedias is that it is a "living document". Anyone, at any time, can write an entry or edit an entry that has already been written. This allows people to correct mistakes and ensures that entries are up-to-date.

Another benefit of Wikipedia is its convenience. You do not have to leave your computer and it is available for free to anyone with an Internet connection. For most other major encyclopedias, like *Encyclopaedia Britannica*, users either have to buy a printed set or pay for an online subscription.

Drawbacks of Wikipedia

However, Wikipedia has its drawbacks – and they can be big ones. Most encyclopedias choose writers who are experts on the topics they cover. On Wikipedia, anyone, including your younger brother, can create an entry, which often results in mistakes. For instance, the day that pop star Michael Jackson died, hundreds of people jumped in to add or change his entry before all of the facts of his death were even available.

Wiki fun facts

1 *Wiki wiki* is the Hawaiian phrase for "quick".

2 About 820,000 people contributed to Wikipedia during March 2007, its biggest month to date. That's a lot of authors and editors!

Michael Jackson's Wikipedia entry was changed hundreds of times the day he died, but only some of the information was true.

Wikipedia editors and alert visitors to the site catch most big errors quickly, but it can sometimes take a few days before they are corrected. Some people deliberately write things that are false or misleading. During election campaigns, for instance, people often exaggerate the accomplishments of the candidates they support or write negative or untrue things about candidates they oppose.

Wikipedia wants YOU

You do not just have to look to Wikipedia as a source. You can also be a contributor. Wikipedia's goal is to "compile the sum of all human knowledge". So, is there a topic that you know a lot about? Snowboarding? West Ham football club?

If there is already a Wikipedia entry about your topic, have a look at it. Do you see any mistakes? Is anything missing? If so, you can edit the entry. If there is no entry on your topic, you can start one. Before you make your mark, you will need to read Wikipedia's tutorial to fully understand the rules and guidelines.

Tips for evaluating a Wikipedia entry

How can you determine whether or not to trust a Wikipedia entry? To help you out, Wikipedia has begun using a feature called WikiTrust, which ranks the "trust levels" of its authors. But you must still be the final judge. Here are some questions to ask yourself:

- **Who wrote the entry?**
  Is the author's name listed on the entry? If not, it could be a bad sign. Why would an author presenting trustworthy information hide his or her identity?
- **Does the entry have citations?**
  How many citations does an entry have? If an entry says, "Dolphins are believed to have no sense of smell", a citation would tell readers the specific book, article, or website this information came from. If an entry has few citations or contains the phrase "citation needed", it may not be trustworthy.
- **What sources are used?**
  How reliable are the sources cited? The National Aeronautics and Space Administration (NASA) might be a great source for an entry on space travel, but the Centre for Space Alien Abductions may be less trustworthy.
- **Just the facts?**
  Make sure the entry sticks to the facts. The statement "Koala bears are marsupials native to Australia" is a fact, but "Koala bears are the cutest animals alive" is someone's opinion. If an entry contains opinions presented as facts, it is probably not trustworthy.

Wikipedia can be a great resource, but it is not 100 per cent foolproof. To get a complete and accurate picture of the topic you are researching, you should make Wikipedia just one source among many that you use. Other resources should include non-fiction books, magazines, atlases, and other websites. Your library's online database provides access to thousands of reliable and user-friendly sites. Remember: even though the information in Wikipedia is not printed on paper, it is still **plagiarism** to copy it without giving credit.

Wikipedia should be only one piece of your research puzzle.

You be the judge

On the Internet, you do not have to be 18 years old to vote. There are thousands of websites where people of any age can make their opinions count. Your ratings, reviews, and **tags** can help others make quality decisions, help you find products you love, and even influence what becomes "front-page" news.

Ratings

For centuries, the **mainstream media** have said that they select the stories that their audiences want to hear. But until recently, the audience really had no way to say which stories interested them the most. The Internet is changing that.

On a website called Digg, visitors share news stories, blogs, or videos from anywhere on the Internet. If enough people "dig" an entry, it is moved to the top. In this way, the readers help determine what becomes "front-page" news. Many online news sources now feature their "most emailed" and "most viewed" stories. This keeps newspapers informed of their readers' tastes, and it keeps readers informed of the day's top stories.

Reviews

In the past, if customers wanted to know about the quality of a book, they had to rely on what the company selling the product said or find a friend who had read it. Or they could trust a critic. Those options are still available.

On the Internet, young people's opinions count just as much as adults'.

Today many online shopping sites allow users to review their products. On the Amazon website, for example, customers can review books and give them a "star ranking". This allows users to read the opinions of hundreds of people around the country.

Tagging

Most radio stations play the songs they want. However, on the Internet, you can personalize your own radio station, based on your preferences. On the music sites Pandora and Last.fm, you can "tag" artists that you like, and the sites will play songs or artists with similar sounds. If you enjoy a song, you can indicate that you liked it so the site will play more songs like it. You can also give feedback that you didn't like a song, which will steer your "station" in a different direction. Many online retailers follow a similar formula, recommending products to you based on ones you have tagged.

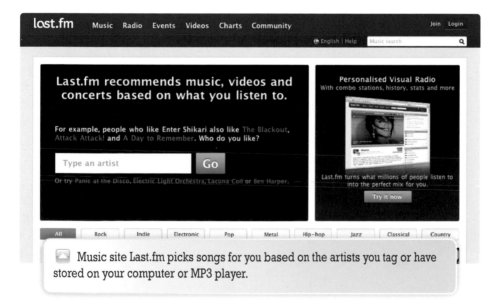

Music site Last.fm picks songs for you based on the artists you tag or have stored on your computer or MP3 player.

It's a matter of trust

Not all opinions are equally good. Most of the users who review films, books, or music are not experts, so be careful whom you believe. You should never trust reviews that contain angry or abusive language. These are "red flags" that a review is not balanced or fair. Also, popularity does not equal quality. Make sure you account for different tastes and levels of experience among reviewers.

A picture is worth a thousand words

SUSAN BOYLE
UNEMPLOYED, 47

If it wasn't for YouTube, Susan Boyle may not have ever become an international singing star. At the very least, her road to success would have been a lot longer!

On 11 April 2009, Susan Boyle, a woman from a small Scottish town, appeared on the television programme *Britain's Got Talent*. Though some people laughed at her appearance, Boyle wowed the audience with a moving and powerful performance of the song "I Dreamed a Dream". The programme was viewed by 10 million people in the United Kingdom.

However, it was not until a video of Boyle's performance was **posted** on YouTube that she became an international sensation. Seventy-two hours after the video was posted, it was watched by 2.5 million people around the world. Within nine days, several videos of Boyle had been viewed a record 100 million times. Since then, Boyle has released a best-selling CD and toured the United States. Boyle has talent, all right, but it was YouTube that provided a global showcase for that talent.

A brief history of YouTube

YouTube is a video-sharing website where users can view videos or post their own. The videos on YouTube range from serious, like footage of two world leaders discussing a war, to silly, like a baby making funny faces. All of the videos are 10 minutes or less, to help prevent people from posting entire television programmes or films, which are often copyrighted (protected from being shown). People who "subscribe" to the website by providing their email addresses can also post videos, become "friends" with other members, and comment on the videos.

Before YouTube was launched in 2005, there was no central place on the Internet for people to store videos. It was also difficult to email videos, as they took up a lot of memory. This made it hard to find videos, or share them. The founders of YouTube wanted to change that, so they came up with the idea of a central place to collect and distribute videos.

Though rankings change every day, YouTube is consistently placed as one of the five most popular websites in the world.

The influence of YouTube

Although YouTube is still somewhat new, it has become an important **media** tool. Here are a few ways it has been and continues to be used.

Politics

Politicians and public figures hoping to reach a wider and younger audience often use YouTube as a way to share their messages. For example, during the 2008 US presidential campaign, 16 of the original 25 candidates chose YouTube as the place to announce their intention to run.

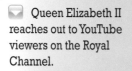
Queen Elizabeth II reaches out to YouTube viewers on the Royal Channel.

YouTube police

YouTube also relies on viewers like you to "police" the website. If you see a video that seems inappropriate, you can "flag" it. Then, a YouTube employee will view it to determine if it violates the site's rules.

Public service

In an effort to curb knife fights in the United Kingdom, in July 2009 the Metropolitan Police released a series of **interactive**, **online** spots on YouTube. The ads feature a short film that can end in different ways, depending on the choices the viewer makes. The videos were popular with young people because, instead of adults telling them what to do, they could see the results of their own choices.

The YOU in YouTube

On the Internet, anyone with a video camera can share recordings with thousands of viewers. In 2007 UK teenager Nick Haley made his own ad for the then-new Apple iPod Touch and posted it on YouTube. The people at Apple loved it, so they invited Nick to their studios and let him remake the ad using professional equipment. Then they broadcast it during top sports programmes!

This is a still frame from the Metropolitan Police's interactive video campaign to stop knife fights.

YouTube for dummies

Creating and posting a video can be fun and easy – sometimes too easy. What seems like a good idea now might not seem so amusing next week, next year, or in five years. So, before you post, pause. Or you could end up like these people.

Two young people in Florida, USA, thought it would be funny to record a mean prank they played at a drive-through restaurant. After getting their drinks, they threw a large soda with ice at the employee. After posting the video on YouTube, the teenagers were arrested and convicted of battery. Their punishment was 100 hours each of community service and a recorded apology broadcast on – where else? – YouTube.

❝ We wanted to create a place where anyone with a video camera, a computer, and an Internet connection can share their life, art, and voice with the world. ❞

– YouTube CEO and co-founder Chad Hurley, talking about YouTube's original aims

Interactive television

On video websites such as Hulu, Dailymotion, Joost, and BBC iPlayer, viewers can watch full-length episodes of network television programmes on their computers, often the day after they air. The programmes are free, although on some websites viewers must sit through ads, which pay for the programme rights.

If YouTube is changing the way we watch videos, these sites are changing the way we watch television. Since viewers can watch what they want, when they want, they no longer have to battle family members for the remote control. With the increasing number of programmes and websites to watch them, many young people do not watch television with a real-life community of people on the sofa. However, sites like Hulu allow viewers to discuss their favourite programmes with fellow fans in **virtual** "viewing rooms" as well as chat boards and forums.

Photo-sharing

When your parents were growing up, it was hard to share photos. People could send photos in the post, but that was expensive, and photos could get bent. Thanks to the Internet, sharing photos is much easier now. All you need is a **digital** camera or mobile phone camera – or even a scanner.

Once you **upload** your photos to a computer, you have many options. You can post photos on a **blog**, email a few to a friend, or post an entire album on a photo-sharing website such as Flickr, Snapfish, Photobucket, or Shutterfly. Facebook has also become a popular place to share photos, since members already have a built-in network of friends and family. (Before you post pictures, make sure you check out the Internet safety advice on page 43.)

Photos that make a difference

You can also email photos of an important event to a news organization. In July 2005, hundreds of people were killed or injured by bombs placed on London's public transport system by terrorists. The BBC asked viewers to send in eyewitness photos of the event, and they received an overwhelming number of photos and videos. Many were published on the BBC website, which helped viewers get a picture of what the event looked like as it unfolded.

📷 Viewers can become "citizen journalists" by submitting their own photos, such as this one of the July 2005 London bombings, to news agencies.

In February 2006, some gruesome photos of US soldiers abusing Iraqi prisoners at a prison called Abu Ghraib were leaked to the media. The photos caused public outrage and forced the US government to address the issue. (See page 50 to read more about "citizen journalists".)

Cyber safety and information overload

With practice and preparation, you can protect yourself from Internet dangers.

Browsing the Internet can be an exciting experience. It can also be scary. With as many as one trillion websites and billions of visitors, you can see things you should not see, hear things you should not hear, and be exposed to strangers you should avoid.

The Internet is a public place. Take the same precautions **online** as you do off-line. Here are some tips to keep you safe:

- **Stranger danger**
  Do not chat with strangers online. These people might not be who they say they are. If someone can find you online and view your information, chances are they can find you off-line, too. Never, ever meet a **cyber** stranger (a stranger you meet in the world of the Internet) in the real world.

- **Privacy, please**
  Never list your phone number, age, address, school, IM name, or last name online. The more information you provide, the more opportunity there is for people to find you or to steal your personal information.

- **Password protection**
  Never pick an obvious password, such as your name, and always use numbers as well as letters. Never, ever share your password – not even with your best friend.

- **Your permanent record**
  Every word you write or photo you **post** could stay on the Internet forever. Even a "private" post can be copied and made public. This can cause you embarrassment and even problems getting hired or admitted to the university of your choice.

- **Cyber bullying**
  Bullying can happen at school or in the park. It can also happen online, especially since your bully can hide his or her identity. If you are the victim of cyber bullying, tell an adult immediately. Mean treatment or abuse should never be tolerated.

Whenever you feel uncomfortable about something on the Internet, talk to an adult. For additional safety information, visit the websites listed on pages 54 and 55.

Information overload (cyber stress)

Can you imagine your life without technology? Most young people spend an average of seven and a half hours each day using a combination of **media**, including mobile phones, MP3 players, computers, video games, the Internet, television, and DVDs. That is about the same as a full-time job! There are also over one trillion websites to compete for your attention on the Internet, with a new one added every minute.

Is your family connected or disconnected by technology?

All of this technology can be a good thing. It can allow you to express yourself, stay connected with people, and find out almost anything with the click of a mouse. However, all of these options can also be stressful. They can even make you ill. You can strain your eyes from staring too long at a computer screen. Or you can find it hard to sleep, as your mind sifts through the information from your day. Some symptoms of "information overload" include eye strain, back pain, relationship stress, inability to focus, inability to make decisions, high blood pressure, headaches, and trouble sleeping.

Fighting information overload

Here are some ways to cope with all the media in your life.

- Stop "multi-tasking". Studies have shown that if you do several things at once, you cannot do each one as well, or even as quickly. Doing one thing at a time also allows you to enjoy or accomplish each project more fully.
- Reboot. Take a break to participate in an activity in which you can engage your body as well as your mind, such as walking, running, or playing a favourite sport.
- Print it out. Print out the pages you are reading on the computer. It will keep you away from Internet distractions and allow you to focus on only one thing. Just make sure you recycle the paper.
- Read a book or magazine. Reading a book or magazine can be a nice escape from the stresses of "cyber overload" and could give your school marks a boost. Studies show that leisure reading of any kind has a more positive impact on your marks than use of any other media.
- Unplug. When you need to concentrate, disable IM or other chat programs that can interrupt you.

" I can't live and hold the camera. **"**

– Canadian rapper Drake, from his song "Say What's Real".

What do you think Drake means by this? If you are always snapping a picture to post on your profile or thinking up your next **status update**, it can be hard to just live in and enjoy the moment. So, put down the camera – and smile for real!

Cyber activism and cyber censorship

With the help of social-networking sites such as Twitter, many thousands of students gathered in Iran's capital of Tehran to protest against the 2009 presidential elections.

An **activist** is someone who works on behalf of a certain cause. The Internet provides tools to help activists do their work. It can help them to plan political **rallies**, gather volunteers, raise money, and raise awareness about unfair situations.

Twitter in Iran

In June 2009, Iran held a presidential election. However, many of Iran's citizens did not believe the results reflected the will of the people. They wanted to show their disapproval and fight for new, fairer elections. Using Twitter on their computers and mobile phones, they organized huge rallies. On Twitter, they were able to share timely news about police crackdowns and arrange new meeting places, if necessary. Because most international reporters had been banned from covering the protests and were sent home, protestors with cameras also took pictures and sent these out to the international community.

Picturing Katrina

When Hurricane Katrina hit the city of New Orleans, USA, in August 2005, some government agencies did not seem to realise how severe the situation was, and they were slow to offer aid to victims. Fortunately, many hurricane survivors took action themselves. They documented the devastating effects of the hurricane with photos and home videos, which they **posted** on websites and emailed to relatives. This helped people to find out how much damage had occurred and respond by sending supplies and rescuers.

Internet censorship

At least 25 countries – including China, Iran, and the Philippines – limit what their citizens can see and say on the Internet. This suppression of information and free speech is called **censorship**. These countries are limiting an important gateway to knowledge. This also leaves a big portion of the population without a real voice. Yet people in these countries fight to be heard.

In 2009 a Cuban blogger, who was known to oppose Cuba's **communist** government, was stopped by undercover officers on her way to a peace rally. She was forced into a car and warned to end her anti-government activities. She suffered bruises but continues to write on her **blog**.

In 2007 an Egyptian blogger was arrested for writing statements critical of **Islam** and the Egyptian government. After a five-minute court hearing, he was sentenced to four years in prison.

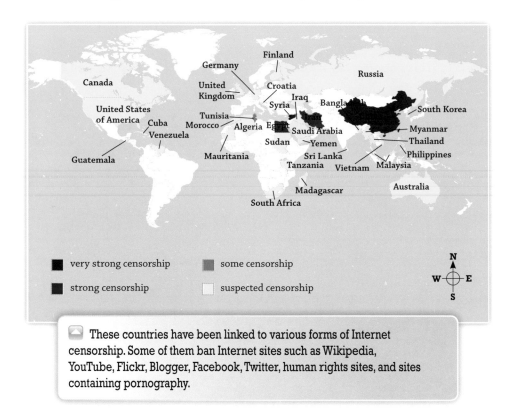

These countries have been linked to various forms of Internet censorship. Some of them ban Internet sites such as Wikipedia, YouTube, Flickr, Blogger, Facebook, Twitter, human rights sites, and sites containing pornography.

Speak up!

Learning about censorship in other countries can help us appreciate our own freedom of speech. While our country may not be perfect, we know that we will not get in trouble for saying so. By voicing our concerns, in fact, we can offer ideas that could help strengthen and improve our nation.

The Internet offers some great tools for letting people express themselves. It is up to you to make your own voice heard.

 ## CASE STUDY: China's Great Firewall

Centuries ago, China built its Great Wall to keep invaders out. More recently, the Chinese government built what is sometimes called "the Great Firewall of China" to restrict the flow of information to and from the country. (A firewall is a computer program that prevents users from accessing information.)

This extensive system of censorship limits what China's 340 million Internet users can read or report. Over 500,000 websites are blocked in China. Here is how Internet censorship works in China.

- The Chinese government employs over 40,000 citizens to monitor emails, blogs, and websites. Employees immediately delete information they consider offensive. They also flood the Internet with pro-government **propaganda**, which are messages aimed to make people form favourable opinions about the government.
- Chinese law requires citizens to use their real names to comment on a website. This helps the government track down people who say things they dislike.
- The Chinese government obtains private information from email providers to track down citizens who violate their laws.
- To do business in China, search engines must remove search results that the Chinese government finds threatening. This includes entries on human rights and certain spiritual practices.

Victory over censorship

In May 2009, a Chinese citizen won a lawsuit over Internet censorship for the first time. Several Chinese software programs also help citizens outwit censorship. Unfortunately, many other countries are starting to import Chinese methods of censorship. So, Internet censorship remains an ongoing battle.

Q & A with the BBC

People formerly known as the "audience" now actively contribute photos or story ideas online. These people are sometimes called "citizen journalists". The BBC News set up an online "hub" to collect photos, videos, and emails from viewers (called "users"). We talked with Patricia Whitehorn from the BBC User-Generated Content (UGC) hub, to learn how citizens contribute to the BBC.

Q: When and why was the User-Generated Content hub set up?
A: Our first real inkling of how powerful users' emails, pictures, and videos could be was during the Asian tsunami in December 2004. But it was the London bombings a few months later, on 7 July 2005, where UGC really came into its own. Passengers trapped on the underground transport system, which was badly affected, were texting us to say something strange was going on – long before any official statement by the emergency services or authorities. Two of the most iconic [well-known] pictures of that day were UGC. The UGC hub was set up then . . . to check and follow up emails, and to look for the best and most newsworthy pictures being sent in to us by the public.

Q: What does the BBC do with the content provided by their readers, listeners, and viewers?
A: The very first thing that we must do, if we receive an email we'd like to follow up, or pictures or video that we'd like to use, is to call the person who sent the material in to us, and make sure it is genuine – this is the verification process. What we are hoping to do more of in the future, is provide cameras and recording equipment to people so they can tell their stories in their own way.

Q: What kind of response has the program received?
A: On an average day, we may receive around 10,000 emails a day, and around 200 to 300 pictures a week, and far fewer videos. But on a breaking news story, the volume for that one story increases dramatically. So on the London 7/7 bombings, we received 22,000 emails and text messages, and 10,000 images by the end of the day.

Timeline

1270 BC The first encyclopedia is written in Syria.

1768 AD *Encyclopaedia Britannica* is published for the first time.

1876 The telephone is **patented** by Alexander Graham Bell.

1944 The world's first **digital** computer is put into public service.

1947 Cells for mobile phone base stations are developed.

1951 Computers are sold commercially for the first time.

1960s The computer mouse is developed.

late 1960s The "Internet" is developed; it is not available to the public.

1973 The first hand-held mobile phone is developed.

1976 Apple I, one of the first affordable home computers, is launched.

1979 The first commercial, fully automated cellular network is launched.

1981 IBM releases an affordable personal computer (PC).
The first laptop computers are sold to the public.

early 1980s The first mobile phone network is launched in the UK.

1989 The World Wide Web is invented.

1990 Internet language (HTML) is created.

1992 The first text message is sent.

1994 The US government releases control of the Internet, and the World Wide Web is opened to the general public.

1997 Robot Wisdom Weblog is published, coining the word *weblog.*

1999 Pyra Labs introduces "Blogger" software.

2001 Wikipedia, the online encyclopedia, is founded.

2004 Facebook is created.

2005 YouTube is launched.
The social-networking site Bebo is launched.

2006 The **micro-blogging** site Twitter is launched.

2008 The video site Hulu is launched.

Glossary

activist someone who works on behalf of a certain cause

blog online diary or journal; short for weblog

censorship practice of suppressing information that a group, such as a government, finds offensive

communist relating to communism, a political system in which a country's economy is controlled by the government

cyber relating to computers

digital data that is broken down into a series of zeros and ones and stored electronically. Computers, MP3 players, CDs, and DVDs all store information digitally.

interactive two-way system of communication, where a user's input affects the system he or she is using

Islam religious faith of Muslims, who believe in a god called Allah and his prophet, Muhammad

journalist professional writer or editor of a news medium

mainstream media major newspapers, magazines, or television networks that reflect commonly accepted views

media means of communication that reach large numbers of people, such as television, newspapers, radio, or Internet websites and blogs

micro-blog short blog containing brief entries about the daily activities of an individual or group

online connected to a computer or computer network

patent to invent a new product or idea; to receive rights to something you have created

plagiarism copying someone else's work without giving credit for it

pornographic sexually explicit material

post transfer information from a computer to another computer or a website

propaganda set of messages aimed at influencing the opinions or behaviour of others

rally gathering to create excitement for a particular cause

status update micro-blogging feature found on social-networking sites that allows users to post news or personal information

tag mark or index information on the Internet

tweet status update posted on Twitter; it must contain 140 characters or less

upload transfer information from a computer to another computer or website

virtual almost existing; existing only online, not in real life

Web 2.0 label for the modern Internet, which contains websites and applications that promote interaction

web portal web page that combines different mini-applications on one page; it serves as an entry point for exploring the Internet

wiki website or web page that can be created or edited in collaboration with other people

Find out more

Books

21st Century Science: Telecoms, Simon Maddison (Franklin Watts, 2007)

Cyber-Safe Kids, Cyber-Savvy Teens: Helping Young People Learn to Use the Internet Safely and Responsibly, Nancy Willard (Jossey-Bass, 2007)

Global Industries Uncovered: The Media and Communications Industry, Rosie Wilson (Wayland, 2009)

Information Literacy Skills (series), Donald C. Adcock (Heinemann Library, 2008)

Child-safe search engines

www.askkids.com
Ask Kids is a safe search engine for young people.

http://kids.yahoo.com
Yahoo! Kids is a safe search engine. It also features games, music, information about films, and more.

Websites

www.direct.gov.uk/en/YoungPeople/CrimeAndJustice/ KeepingSafe/DG_10027670
This website deals with online safety, including information about cyber bullying on social-networking sites and the dangers of chat rooms.

www.thinkuknow.co.uk/11_16/
Have a look at this website to learn about staying safe online and what new sites are good to visit.

www.volunteergenie.org.uk/new-media-adventures
This website contains some useful information about social-networking sites, blogging and citizen journalism.

www.kidsmart.org.uk
Learn more about Internet safety on this website.

http://news.bbc.co.uk/2/hi/talking_point/default.stm
This BBC website allows ordinary people to report the news as it happens.

Topics to research

To learn more about the Internet, research the following topics:
- the invention and development of the Internet
- privacy and security issues surrounding personal information on social-networking sites
- Internet censorship versus freedom of speech: what are the arguments used to support each side?

Index